OAKLAND RAIDERS · SUPER BOWL CHAMPIONS

XI, JANUARY 9, 1977
32-14 VERSUS MINNESOTA VIKINGS

XV, JANUARY 25, 1981
27-10 VERSUS PHILADELPHIA EAGLES

XVIII, JANUARY 22, 1984
38-9 VERSUS WASHINGTON REDSKINS

SUPER BOWL CHAMPIONS

OAKLAND RAIDERS

AARON FRISCH

CREATIVE EDUCATION

COVER: RUNNING BACK MARCUS ALLEN

PAGE 2: GUARD GENE UPSHAW RESTING BETWEEN PLAYS

RIGHT: OFFENSIVE TACKLE ROBERT GALLERY BLOCKING

Published by Creative Education
P.O. Box 227, Mankato, Minnesota 56002
Creative Education is an imprint of The Creative Company
www.thecreativecompany.us

Book and cover design by Blue Design (www.bluedes.com)
Art direction by Rita Marshall
Printed by Corporate Graphics in the United States of
America

Photographs by Corbis (Bettmann), Dreamstime (Rosco),
Getty Images (Stephen Dunn, John Elk III, James Flores/
NFL, Paul Jasienski, George Long/NFL, John G. Mabanglo/
AFP, Al Messerschmidt/NFL, Ronald C. Modra/Sports
Imagery, NFL/NFL, Mike Powell, Greg Trott, Michael
Zagaris)

Library of Congress Cataloging-in-Publication Data

Frisch, Aaron.
Oakland Raiders / by Aaron Frisch.
p. cm. — (Super Bowl champions)
Includes index.
Summary: An elementary look at the Oakland Raiders
professional football team, including its formation in 1960,
most memorable players, Super Bowl championships, and
stars of today.
ISBN 978-1-60818-025-7
1. Oakland Raiders (Football team)—History—Juvenile
literature. I. Title. II. Series.

GV956.O24F75 2011
796.332'640979466—dc22   2010001022

CPSIA: 040110 PO1141

First Edition
9 8 7 6 5 4 3 2 1

CONTENTS

SUPER BOWL CHAMPIONS

Oakland is a city in California. Oakland is an important **port** along the Pacific Ocean. It has a **stadium** called Oakland-Alameda County Coliseum that is the home of a football team called the Raiders.

... OAKLAND WAS BUILT NEXT TO WATER SO SHIPS COULD GET THERE ...

RAIDERS FACTS

First season:
1960

Conference/division:
American Football Conference, West Division

Super Bowl championships:
XI, January 9, 1977 / 32-14 versus Minnesota Vikings
XV, January 25, 1981 / 27-10 versus Philadelphia Eagles
XVIII, January 22, 1984 / 38-9 versus Washington
Redskins

Training camp location:
Napa Valley, California

NFL Web site for kids:
http://nflrush.com

The Raiders are part of the National Football League (NFL). All the teams in the NFL try to win the Super Bowl to become world champions. The Raiders' uniforms are black and silver. One of their main **rivals** is the Denver Broncos.

... MANY RAIDERS FANS LIKE TO DRESS UP IN BLACK AND SILVER ...

SUPER BOWL CHAMPIONS

The Raiders played their first season in 1960. They were part of a different **league** called the American Football League then. In 1963, the Raiders hired coach Al Davis. He became the owner of the team, too.

... AL DAVIS HELPED MAKE OAKLAND A TOUGH TEAM IN THE 1960S ...

11

SUPER BOWL CHAMPIONS

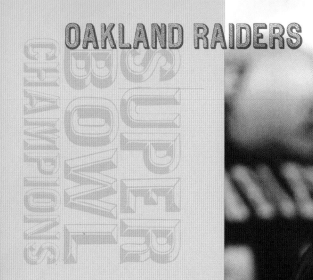

Say It Like This

Biletnikoff:
bih-LET-nih-kahf

In 1965, the Raiders got a
wide receiver named Fred
Biletnikoff. In 1969, they
hired a new coach named
John Madden. After the
1976 season, Biletnikoff and
Madden helped the Raiders
win Super Bowl XI (11).

12

With new quarterback Jim Plunkett, the Raiders won Super Bowl XV (15). In 1982, the Raiders moved to the city of Los Angeles. They won Super Bowl XVIII (18) the next year. In 1995, the Raiders moved back to Oakland.

... FRED BILETNIKOFF (LEFT) AND JIM PLUNKETT (RIGHT) ...

OAKLAND RAIDERS

SUPER BOWL CHAMPIONS

14

... FANS SOMETIMES CALLED TIM BROWN "TOUCHDOWN TIMMY" ...

SUPER BOWL CHAMPIONS

The Raiders had some good seasons in the 1990s. Then, players like wide receiver Tim Brown helped Oakland get to Super Bowl XXXVII (37). But this time, the Raiders lost.

Two of the Raiders' first stars were Jim Otto and Willie Brown. Otto was a tough center who wore number 00 on his jersey. Brown was a fast cornerback who made 39 total interceptions. That is a team **record**.

... JIM OTTO (LEFT) AND WILLIE BROWN (RIGHT) ...

17

WHY ARE THEY CALLED THE RAIDERS?

The first owners of the Oakland team wanted a name that sounded tough. "Raiders" is another name for pirates. Pirates are tough sailors who sail on the ocean and try to steal treasure.

Versatile running back Marcus Allen joined the Raiders in 1982. He used slick moves to get away from tacklers. Howie Long was another Raiders star. He was a big defensive end who led the defense for 13 seasons.

... HOWIE LONG WAS A STRONG AND FAST DEFENSIVE LINEMAN ...

... FANS LIKED TO WATCH NNAMDI ASOMUGHA RACE ACROSS THE FIELD ...

The Raiders added cornerback Nnamdi Asomugha in 2003. He covered other teams' best wide receivers. Oakland fans hoped that he would help lead the Raiders to their fourth Super Bowl championship!

21

SUPER
BOWL
CHAMPIONS

SUPER BOWL CHAMPIONS

GLOSSARY

league — a group of teams that all play against each other

port — a city along an ocean or big lake where ships pick up and drop off goods

record — something that is the best or most ever

rivals — teams that play extra hard against each other

stadium — a large building that has a sports field and many seats for fans

versatile (*VER-suh-tul*) — good at doing many things, like running, blocking, and catching passes

SUPER BOWL CHAMPIONS

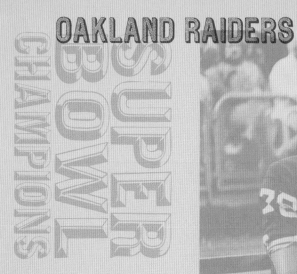

24

INDEX